JOHN BURNINGHAM

Would You Rather...

SeaStar Books
NEW YORK

First published in 1978 by Jonathan Cape, The Random House Group Limited, London

SeaStar Books
A division of North-South Books Inc.

Published in the United States in 2002 by SeaStar Books, a division of North-South Books Inc., New York.
First SeaStar Books paperback edition published in 2003.

Library of Congress Cataloging-in-Publication Data
Burningham, John.
Would you rather— / John Burningham
p. cm.
Summary: A series of comical choices such as, "Would you rather eat spider stew or slug dumplings or mashed worms?" ends with an invitation to bedtime.
[1. Bedtime—Fiction. 2. Decision making—Fiction. 3. Humorous stories] I. Title
PZ7.B936 Wo 2002
[E]—dc21

ISBN 1-58717-135-X (reinforced trade edition)
1 3 5 7 9 RTE 10 8 6 4 2
ISBN 1-58717-217-8 (paperback edition)
1 3 5 7 9 PB 10 8 6 4 2

Printed in Singapore

For more information about our books, and the authors and artists who create them, visit our web site: www.northsouth.com

Would you rather . . .

your **HOUSE** were surrounded by

WATER

SNOW

or **JUNGLE**?

Would you rather . . .

an **ELEPHANT** drank your **BATHWATER**

an **EAGLE**
stole your **DINNER**

a **PIG** tried on your **CLOTHES**

or a **HIPPO** slept in your **BED**?

Would you rather be . . .

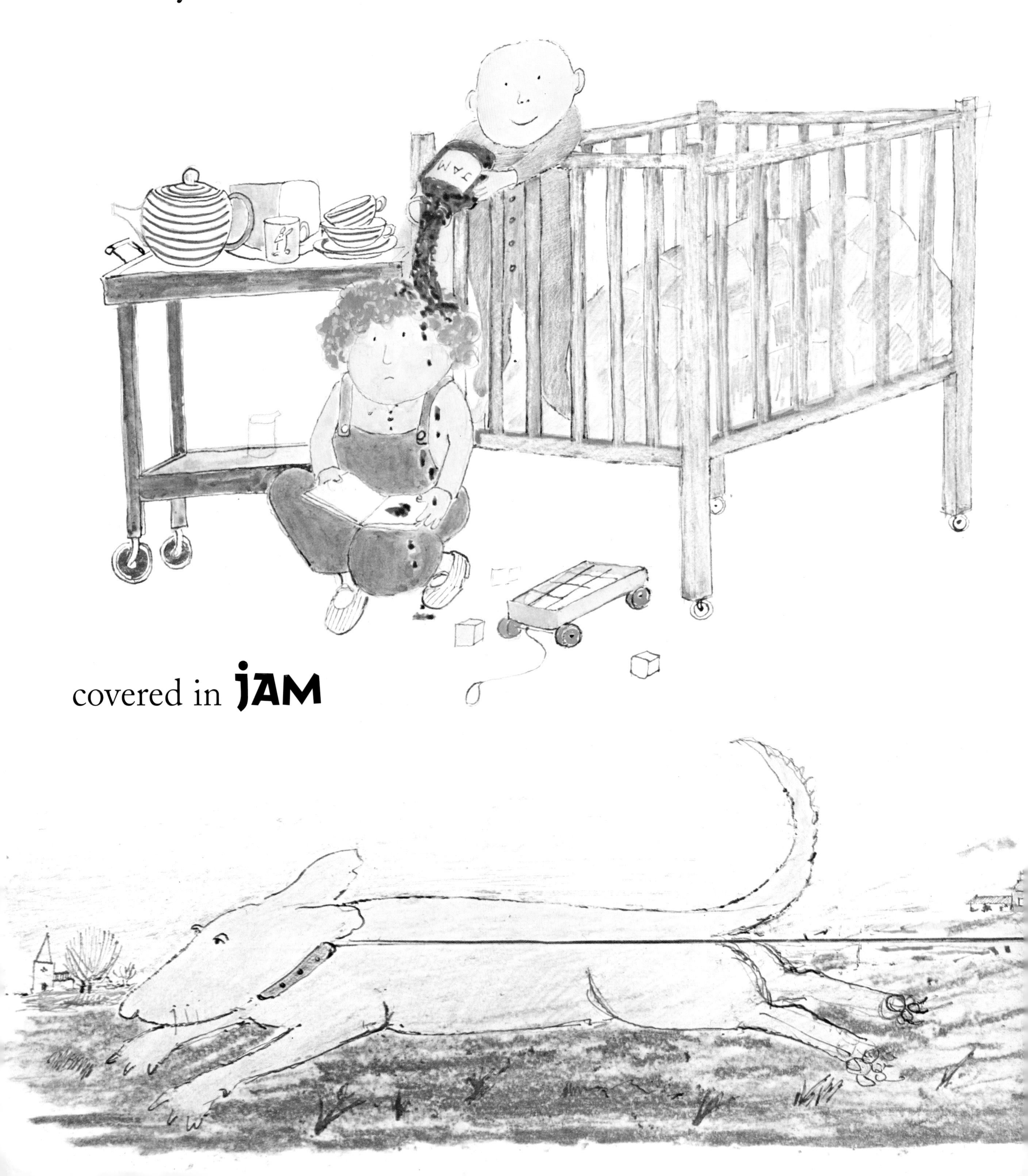

covered in **JAM**

SOAKED
with water

or pulled through the **MUD** by a dog?

Would you rather have . . .

supper in a **CASTLE**

breakfast in a **BALLOON**

or tea on the **RIVER**?

Would you rather be made to . . .

eat **SPIDER** stew

taste **SLUG** dumplings

chew mashed
WORMS

or drink
a **SNAIL**
shake?

Would you rather . . .

JUMP in the **NETTLES** for five dollars

SWALLOW a dead **FROG** for twenty dollars

or stay all night in a

CREEPY HOUSE

for fifty dollars?

Would you rather be . . .

CRUSHED by a **SNAKE**

SWALLOWED by a **FISH**

EATEN by a **CROCODILE**

or **SAT ON** by a **RHINOCEROS**?

Would you rather . . .

your **DAD** did a **DANCE** at school

or your **MOM** made a **FUSS** in a café?

Would you rather . . .

CLASH two cymbals

BANG a drum

or **BLOW** a trumpet?

Would you rather . . .

TICKLE a monkey

READ to a koala

BOX with a cat

SKATE with a dog

RIDE on a pig

or **DANCE** with a goat?

Would you rather be **CHASED** by . . .

a **CRAB**

a **BULL**

a **LION**

or **WOLVES**?

Or would you like to

into a supermarket?

3p OFF
3p OFF
3p OFF
3p OFF
SPECIAL OFFER
THIS WEEK
Sunny Sip
Sunny Sip

Would you rather be **LOST** . . .

in the **FOG**

at **SEA**

in a **DESERT**

in a **FOREST**

or in a **CROWD**?

Would you rather help . . .

a **FAIRY** make magic

GNOMES dig for treasure

an **IMP** be naughty

a **WITCH** make stew

or **SANTA CLAUS** deliver presents?

Would you rather live with . . .

a **GERBIL** in a cage

a **FISH** in a bowl

a **PARROT** on a perch

a **RABBIT** in a hutch

CHICKENS in a coop

or a **DOG** in a kennel?

Or perhaps you would rather
just go to sleep in
YOUR OWN BED!